Mom's Boot Camp Journal

Training Starts:

_____

Graduation:

_____

The night your recruit arrives at the Recruit Depot, you will receive a phone call stating he/she has arrived safely.

You will not hear from them again until you receive a letter in the mail approximately 3-5 days later. This letter will contain a form letter from the Senior Drill Instructor and will have your recruits address. At this time you will be able to start sending your recruit letters. Here is what the address will look like.

Parris Island

Example:
RCT Joe Smith
1st RCTBN A Co PLT 1086
PO Box 16945
Parris Island, SC 29905

San Diego

Example:
RCT Joe Smith
1st RCTBN A Co PLT 1086
4004 Midway Ave
San Diego, CA 92140

May your future Marine be blessed with safety and health through their tour of duty; starting now with their journey through recruit training.

We hope you will use this journal as a growth tool. You will experience many emotions with your recruit going through this. Writing things down will make a difference in how you feel about the situation. Always keep your letters to your recruit positive! If you have negative feelings about their absence, write them here! Not in the letters to your recruit!

We would recommend searching Facebook for the Marine Parents group. It's a great group made up of Marines and parents of Marines. People that are at the graduations take pictures of recruits in training and will post them on the pages. You'll find yourself scouring the page daily looking for pictures of your "Waldo". They call them that because they all look the same.

Good luck, and

SEMPER FIDELIS

Training Day _____ Date_____

Good Morning

Good Evening

_____
_____
_____
_____
_____
_____
_____
_____
_____

Training Day _____ Date_____

Good Morning

Good Evening

_____
_____
_____
_____
_____
_____
_____
_____
_____

Training Day _____ Date_____

Good Morning

Good Evening

_____

_____

_____

_____

_____

_____

_____

_____

_____

Training Day _____ Date_____

Good Morning

Good Evening

_____
_____
_____
_____
_____
_____
_____
_____
_____

Training Day _____ Date_____

Good Morning

Good Evening

_____
_____
_____
_____
_____
_____
_____
_____
_____

Training Day _____ Date_____

Good Morning

Good Evening

_____
_____
_____
_____
_____
_____
_____
_____
_____

Training Day _____ Date_____

Good Morning

Good Evening

_____

_____

_____

_____

_____

_____

_____

_____

_____

_____

Training Day _____ Date_____

Good Morning

Good Evening

_____
_____
_____
_____
_____
_____
_____
_____
_____

Training Day _____ Date_____

Good Morning

Good Evening

_____
_____
_____
_____
_____
_____
_____
_____

Training Day _____ Date_____

Good Morning

Good Evening

_____
_____
_____
_____
_____
_____
_____
_____
_____

Training Day _____ Date_____

Good Morning

Good Evening

_____
_____
_____
_____
_____
_____
_____
_____
_____

Training Day _____ Date_____

Good Morning

Good Evening

_____
_____
_____
_____
_____
_____
_____
_____
_____

Training Day _____ Date_____

Good Morning

Good Evening

_____
_____
_____
_____
_____
_____
_____
_____

Training Day _____ Date_____

Good Morning

Good Evening

_____
_____
_____
_____
_____
_____
_____
_____
_____

Training Day _____ Date_____

Good Morning

Good Evening

_____
_____
_____
_____
_____
_____
_____
_____
_____

Training Day _____ Date_____

Good Morning

Good Evening

_____
_____
_____
_____
_____
_____
_____
_____
_____

Training Day _____ Date_____

Good Morning

Good Evening

_____
_____
_____
_____
_____
_____
_____
_____
_____

Training Day _____ Date_____

Good Morning

Good Evening

_____
_____
_____
_____
_____
_____
_____
_____
_____

Training Day _____ Date_____

Good Morning

Good Evening

_____
_____
_____
_____
_____
_____
_____
_____
_____

Training Day _____ Date_____

Good Morning

Good Evening

_____
_____
_____
_____
_____
_____
_____
_____
_____

Training Day _____ Date_____

Good Morning

Good Evening

_____
_____
_____
_____
_____
_____
_____
_____
_____

Training Day _____ Date_____

Good Morning

Good Evening

_____
_____
_____
_____
_____
_____
_____
_____

Training Day _____ Date_____

Good Morning

Good Evening

_____

_____

_____

_____

_____

_____

_____

_____

_____

Training Day _____ Date_____

Good Morning

Good Evening

_____
_____
_____
_____
_____
_____
_____
_____

Training Day _____ Date_____

Good Morning

Good Evening

_____
_____
_____
_____
_____
_____
_____
_____
_____
_____

Training Day _____ Date_____

Good Morning

Good Evening

Training Day _____ Date_____

Good Morning

Good Evening

_____
_____
_____
_____
_____
_____
_____
_____
_____

Training Day _____ Date_____

Good Morning

Good Evening

_____
_____
_____
_____
_____
_____
_____
_____
_____

Training Day _____ Date_____

Good Morning

Good Evening

Training Day _____ Date_____

Good Morning

Good Evening

_____
_____
_____
_____
_____
_____
_____
_____
_____

Training Day _____ Date _____

Good Morning

Good Evening

_____
_____
_____
_____
_____
_____
_____
_____
_____

Training Day _____ Date_____

Good Morning

Good Evening

Training Day _____ Date_____

Good Morning

Good Evening

_____
_____
_____
_____
_____
_____
_____
_____

Training Day _____ Date_____

Good Morning

Good Evening

_____
_____
_____
_____
_____
_____
_____
_____
_____

Training Day _____ Date_____

Good Morning

Good Evening

_____
_____
_____
_____
_____
_____
_____
_____
_____

Training Day _____ Date_____

Good Morning

Good Evening

_____

_____

_____

_____

_____

_____

_____

_____

_____

Training Day _____ Date_____

Good Morning

Good Evening

_____
_____
_____
_____
_____
_____
_____
_____
_____

Training Day _____ Date_____

Good Morning

Good Evening

_____
_____
_____
_____
_____
_____
_____
_____

Training Day _____ Date_____

Good Morning

Good Evening

_____
_____
_____
_____
_____
_____
_____
_____
_____

Training Day _____ Date_____

Good Morning

Good Evening

_____
_____
_____
_____
_____
_____
_____
_____

Training Day _____ Date_____

Good Morning

Good Evening

_____
_____
_____
_____
_____
_____
_____
_____
_____

Training Day _____ Date_____

Good Morning

Good Evening

Training Day _____ Date_____

Good Morning

Good Evening

_____
_____
_____
_____
_____
_____
_____
_____
_____

Training Day _____ Date_____

Good Morning

Good Evening

_____
_____
_____
_____
_____
_____
_____
_____
_____

Training Day _____ Date_____

Good Morning

Good Evening

_____
_____
_____
_____
_____
_____
_____
_____
_____

Training Day _____ Date_____

Good Morning

Good Evening

_____
_____
_____
_____
_____
_____
_____
_____
_____

Training Day _____ Date_____

Good Morning

Good Evening

_____
_____
_____
_____
_____
_____
_____
_____
_____

Training Day _____ Date_____

Good Morning

Good Evening

_____
_____
_____
_____
_____
_____
_____
_____
_____

Training Day _____ Date_____

Good Morning

Good Evening

_____
_____
_____
_____
_____
_____
_____
_____
_____

Training Day _____ Date_____

Good Morning

Good Evening

_____
_____
_____
_____
_____
_____
_____
_____
_____

Training Day _____ Date_____

Good Morning

Good Evening

_____
_____
_____
_____
_____
_____
_____
_____
_____

Training Day _____ Date_____

Good Morning

Good Evening

_____

_____

_____

_____

_____

_____

_____

_____

_____

Training Day _____ Date_____

Good Morning

Good Evening

_____
_____
_____
_____
_____
_____
_____
_____

Training Day _____ Date_____

Good Morning

Good Evening

Training Day _____ Date_____

Good Morning

Good Evening

_____
_____
_____
_____
_____
_____
_____
_____
_____

Training Day _____ Date_____

Good Morning

Good Evening

_____
_____
_____
_____
_____
_____
_____
_____

Training Day _____ Date_____

Good Morning

Good Evening

_____
_____
_____
_____
_____
_____
_____
_____
_____

Training Day _____ Date_____

Good Morning

Good Evening

_____
_____
_____
_____
_____
_____
_____
_____
_____

Training Day _____ Date_____

Good Morning

Good Evening

_____
_____
_____
_____
_____
_____
_____
_____
_____

Training Day _____ Date_____

Good Morning

Good Evening

_____
_____
_____
_____
_____
_____
_____
_____
_____

Training Day _____ Date_____

Good Morning

Good Evening

_____
_____
_____
_____
_____
_____
_____
_____
_____

Training Day _____ Date_____

Good Morning

Good Evening

_____

_____

_____

_____

_____

_____

_____

_____

_____

Training Day _____ Date_____

Good Morning

Good Evening

_____
_____
_____
_____
_____
_____
_____
_____
_____

Training Day _____ Date_____

Good Morning

Good Evening

_____

_____

_____

_____

_____

_____

_____

_____

_____

Training Day _____ Date_____

Good Morning

Good Evening

_____

_____

_____

_____

_____

_____

_____

_____

_____

Training Day _____ Date_____

Good Morning

Good Evening

_____
_____
_____
_____
_____
_____
_____
_____
_____
_____

Training Day _____ Date_____

Good Morning

Good Evening

_____
_____
_____
_____
_____
_____
_____
_____

Training Day _____ Date_____

Good Morning

Good Evening

_____
_____
_____
_____
_____
_____
_____
_____
_____

Training Day _____ Date_____

Good Morning

Good Evening

_____
_____
_____
_____
_____
_____
_____
_____

Training Day _____ Date_____

Good Morning

Good Evening

_____
_____
_____
_____
_____
_____
_____
_____

Training Day _____ Date_____

Good Morning

Good Evening

Training Day _____ Date_____

Good Morning

Good Evening

_____
_____
_____
_____
_____
_____
_____
_____
_____
_____

Training Day _____ Date_____

Good Morning

Good Evening

_____
_____
_____
_____
_____
_____
_____
_____
_____

Training Day _____ Date_____

Good Morning

Good Evening

_____
_____
_____
_____
_____
_____
_____
_____
_____

Training Day _____ Date_____

Good Morning

Good Evening

Training Day _____ Date_____

Good Morning

Good Evening

_____
_____
_____
_____
_____
_____
_____
_____

Training Day _____ Date_____

Good Morning

Good Evening

_____
_____
_____
_____
_____
_____
_____
_____
_____

Training Day _____ Date_____

Good Morning

Good Evening

_____
_____
_____
_____
_____
_____
_____
_____

Training Day _____ Date_____

Good Morning

Good Evening

_____
_____
_____
_____
_____
_____
_____
_____
_____

Training Day _____ Date_____

Good Morning

Good Evening

_____
_____
_____
_____
_____
_____
_____
_____
_____

Training Day _____ Date_____

Good Morning

Good Evening

_____
_____
_____
_____
_____
_____
_____
_____
_____

Training Day _____ Date_____

Good Morning

Good Evening

_____
_____
_____
_____
_____
_____
_____
_____

Training Day _____ Date_____

Good Morning

Good Evening

Training Day _____ Date_____

Good Morning

Good Evening

_____
_____
_____
_____
_____
_____
_____
_____
_____

Training Day _____ Date_____

Good Morning

Good Evening

_____
_____
_____
_____
_____
_____
_____
_____
_____

Training Day _____ Date_____

Good Morning

Good Evening

_____
_____
_____
_____
_____
_____
_____
_____
_____

Training Day _____ Date_____

Good Morning

Good Evening

_____
_____
_____
_____
_____
_____
_____
_____
_____

Training Day _____ Date_____

Good Morning

Good Evening

_____
_____
_____
_____
_____
_____
_____
_____
_____

Training Day _____ Date_____

Good Morning

Good Evening

_____
_____
_____
_____
_____
_____
_____
_____
_____

Training Day _____ Date_____

Good Morning

Good Evening

_____

_____

_____

_____

_____

_____

_____

_____

Training Day _____ Date_____

Good Morning

Good Evening

_____
_____
_____
_____
_____
_____
_____
_____

Training Day _____ Date_____

Good Morning

Good Evening

_____
_____
_____
_____
_____
_____
_____
_____
_____

Made in United States
North Haven, CT
25 July 2022

21835090R00057